MORE UKULELE MAGIC

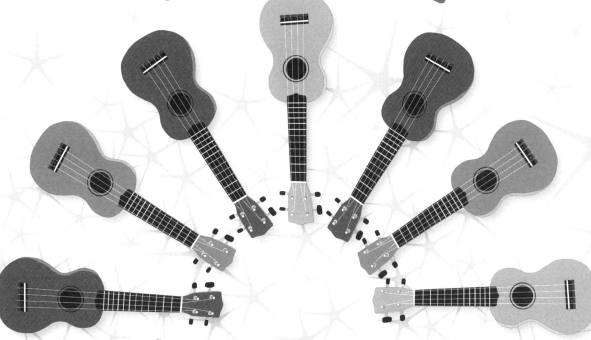

IAN LAWRENCE

Collins MUSIC

Downloadable content

Use the link below to access printable scores and a whiteboard e-book with full video and audio support:

www.collins.co.uk/ukulelemagicTB/download

First published 2020
Published by Collins, an imprint of HarperCollins*Publishers* Ltd
The News Building
1 London Bridge Street
London
SE1 9GF

www.collins.co.uk

10 9 8 7 6 5 4 3 2 1

ISBN: 978-0-00-839471-4

Text and music © 2020 Ian Lawrence

Special thanks to Trevor Sheldrake and Alastair Thompson

Printed by Caligraving Ltd, Thetford, Norfolk
Cover design by Saffron Stocker
Designed by Ken Vail Graphic Design Ltd
Vocals performed by Louise Victoria, Zach Said and Ian Lawrence
Recorded at Berners Street Studio, engineered by Jonas Persson
Filmed by Alex Evans, edited by Berlin

MIX
Paper from
responsible sources
FSC C007454

This book is produced from independently certified FSC paper to ensure responsible forest management.

For more information visit: **www.harpercollins.co.uk/green**

Contents

Welcome to More Ukulele Magic

Diagrams show what strings to play and where to put your fingers.

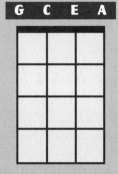

Use the tuning track to tune your ukulele strings:

Audio 1 (tuning track)

More Ukulele Magic: Tutor Book 2 extends and builds on the techniques and skills in *Ukulele Magic: Tutor Book 1* with fun activities and songs for young ukulele players. The first page of each unit outlines the learning objectives and provides useful background information to help you prepare.

Audio support

The CD provides a demo and backing track for every song and instrumental piece in the book. Choose to sing or play along with the demo for support or go solo with the backing track. The audio icons ● tell you which tracks to play for each song (the demo track 'd' will come first, followed by the backing track 'b'). Where needed, backing tracks start with percussion 'count-in' beats so that you know when to start playing. Track 1 is the tuning track, for tuning the ukulele to the correct pitch (the diagram on the left shows which notes you will tune to).

Scores and notation

Scores are included with both the teacher and pupil editions and are available online. Lead sheets (with melody line, chord names and main song lyrics) are provided for every song. Major chords are written with the letter name only (e.g. C); minor chords are written with a small 'm' (e.g. Cm). TAB sheets are provided for songs and pieces featuring ukulele melodies. See page 2 for instructions on how to access downloadable content.

Teacher's edition and video support

The teacher's edition includes downloadable videos for each unit, demonstrating new strumming patterns and techniques. These are embedded along with the audio tracks and scores in a whiteboard e-book – ideal for whole-class settings. Navigate using these buttons ●●●, click on the video icon ● to watch a demonstration, use the audio icons ● to hear the demo and backing tracks, and click on the scores icon ● to see the notation. See page 2 for instructions on how to access downloadable content.

On Track

Important information about the audio tracks, such as the length of the introduction.

Audio X (d)
Play demo track

Audio X (b)
Play backing track

Video X
View video support

Scores
View or print notation

Finger tips

- The Fingertips text tells you what you need to know to play well.

Challenge

- The Challenge text offers ideas for extension activities.

UNIT 1
MORE STRUMMING TRICKS

Things to remember:

- The basic strum used in this unit is the shuffle strum from songs like 'The Rocky Mountain Line' in *Ukulele Magic: Tutor Book 1*.

- 'N.C.' means 'no chord'. You should stop strumming when you see this symbol.

TWO SONGS TO SING, RAP AND PLAY

Back Beat Rap

Ukulele Boogie Woogie

In this section you will:

- Play the accented shuffle strum
- Play a boogie woogie shuffle strum
- Learn about altering notes in a chord
- Play the new chords G (major), D minor and E minor, and two versions of the new chord D7

Good to know...

Back Beat Rap

- As with all ukulele chords, D7 can be formed in several ways. There are two versions of D7 shown here: a simpler version where only two strings are fretted, and a second version where three of the strings are held down by the first finger laying flat across them – this is known as a barre chord.

- A 'riff' is a repeated fragment of melody, usually instrumental. A riff can be played as part of an accompaniment. In 'Back Beat Rap' it is played between the verses.

Ukulele Boogie Woogie

- The shuffle strum can be played in a 'straight' style, where all the strums are of equal length in a 'chug-ga, chug-ga, chug-ga, chug-ga' pattern.

- In a 'swing' shuffle, the down strums are played slightly longer in the 'doo-bee, doo-bee, doo-bee, doo-bee' pattern commonly found in jazz.

Back Beat Rap

More strumming tricks

(A rap song with riffs)

D7	D7 (barre)

Drum and bass introduction
ONE, TWO, THREE, FOUR! Make it just a little stronger
On the TWO and on the FOUR, just like a RAP beat on the BACK beat.

Repeat on ukulele using the strumming patterns shown by the arrows:

D7   D7

ONE, TWO, THREE, FOUR! Make it just a lit-tle strong-er

D7   D7

On the TWO and on the FOUR, just like a RAP beat on the BACK beat.

INSTRUMENTAL RIFF – *D7 accented shuffle (4 bars/16 beats)*
D7

1   +   2   +   3   +   4   +

On Track

There is a 2-bar (8-beat) drum and bass introduction before the first rap. There are no ukulele strums during the rap sections.

page 6

Audio 2 (d)

Audio 3 (b)

Video

Scores

Finger tips

- The first version of D7 is easy to play. The second version is a barre chord shape. This means that you hold down all four strings at the second fret by laying your first finger flat across them. With your second finger, hold down the first string at the third fret.

Back Beat Rap (continued)

(A rap song with riffs)

Back in the day, the drummer in a band
Said a strong beat one was not much fun
And so he hit the snare drum on the two and the four,
The crowd went 'wow', they shouted out for more.

INSTRUMENTAL RIFF – *D7 accented shuffle (4 bars/16 beats)*
D7

Pretty soon this back-beat fashion became quite a passion
And every kind of music had a ration,
From pop to hip-hop; ev'ry kind of song,
You're gonna find a strong back beat going on.

INSTRUMENTAL RIFF – *D7 accented shuffle (8 bars/32 beats)*
D7

Challenge

- (Teacher) Use the video clip to help you create some ukulele percussion to accompany a live performance.
- Play the solo ukulele riff written on the TAB sheet or create your own riff using the D blues scale (see Unit 7, 'Making It Up').
- Create your own original rap to the backing track. You could choose a seasonal topic like 'Christmas Rapping' for instance.

Ukulele Boogie Woogie

More strumming tricks

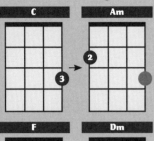
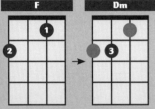
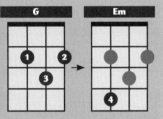

(A boogie woogie song)

C　　(Am)　　C　　N.C.　　F　　(Dm)　　F　　N.C.

↓　↑　↓　↑　↓　　　↓　↑　↓　↑　↓

Boo - gie woo - gie high,　　boo - gie woo - gie low,
　　　　Get up　　　　　　　　　and

C　　(Am)　　C　　(Am)　　C　　(Am)　　C　　N.C.

↓　↑　↓　↑　↓　↑　↓　↑　↓　↑　↓　↑　↓

Boo - gie woo - gie rhy - thm makes the boo - gie woo - gie flow.
go!

F　　(Dm)　　F　　N.C.　F　　(Dm)　　F　　N.C.
Boogie woogie blues,　　boogie woogie soul.
　　　　Get up　　　　　　　　and

C　　(Am)　C　　(Am)　C　　(Am)　C　　N.C.
Boogie woogie jazz or boogie woogie rock and roll.
go!

On Track

There is a 2-bar (8-beat) introduction. The piece is played 3 times.

page 8

Audio 4 (d)　Audio 5 (b)

Video　Scores

Fingertips

● When changing the chord on the 'back beat' (for example C to Am or G to Em), hold the original chord shape in place and just add one finger to alter the chord, as shown in the chord diagrams. This means that some chords will be fretted slightly differently to normal, but they will be easier and smoother to play.

● Practise the chord changes slowly at first and gradually increase the speed.

● (Teacher) The video clip provides a demonstration.

Ukulele Boogie Woogie (continued)

(A boogie woogie song)

```
G     (Em)    G        N.C.   F   (Am) F        N.C.
Boogie Woogie Night:           Uku-lele   Show.
                       Get up                   and

C  (Am) C      (Am)     C       (Am)    C   N.C.
Uku-lele boogie woogie! Let's get up and go!
go!
```

Shuffle strum

Boo - gie woo - gie high

Challenge

● Experiment altering some other chords by holding down or releasing one of the strings. For example, lift your first finger on and off while strumming the A chord to alternate between A and A minor.

● Learn to play and/or sing the second part ('Get up and go!'). The notes are given in the lead sheet and the TAB sheet, and can be heard on the demo track.

UNIT 2
POPPING AROUND THE WORLD

Things to remember:

- The reggae strums are more effective if the strings are 'damped' with the side of your strumming hand between each chord. This gives each chord a short, tidy sound instead of allowing the strings to ring. We used this technique in *Ukulele Magic: Tutor Book 1* in the song 'A Minor Miracle'.

TWO SONGS TO SING AND PLAY

Take It Easy

Samba Lele

In this section you will:

- Explore some musical styles from around the world
- Play two reggae strum patterns
- Play a ukulele samba strum and some ukulele samba percussion
- Play the new chords B♭ (major), G minor and A7
- Play the roll strum

Good to know...

Take It Easy

- The reggae style of music developed in Jamaica before it became world famous in the 1970s, notably through the music of Bob Marley and the Wailers. The song 'Take It Easy' is written in a reggae style with similar chord progressions to the ones used by Bob Marley.

Samba Lele

- Samba is not only the exciting, loud music associated with carnival processions in the street; in Brazil, people play a quieter style known as 'Cafe Samba' where you can imagine the rhythms being created by shaking a jar of sugar or tapping a coffee cup with a spoon.

- 'Samba Lele' is a famous Brazilian song. Some of the words are in Portuguese, the language of Brazil. 'Favelas' are the areas of crowded and typically poorly-built housing in big cities like Rio de Janeiro. Many favelas have a Samba School, or 'Escola de Samba' where, every year, local people prepare samba music with dancers in elaborate costumes for the Rio Carnival.

Take It Easy

Popping around the world

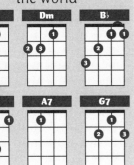

Dm   B♭

A7   G7

(A reggae song)

CHORUS

N.C.   F   Dm
Take it easy,

B♭   F
No more rushing a-round.

         F   Dm
Take it easy, the beach is waiting,

   B♭   F
The sun is shining down.

VERSE

Dm   Dm
    Monday morning till Friday night,

Gm   A7
Working hard, gotta earn your pay.

Dm   Dm
    Now the weekend has come in sight,

G7   C   N.C.
Get a break, have a holiday.

CHORUS
Reggae strum 1

1 + 2 + 3 + 4 +

VERSE
Reggae strum 2

1 + 2 + 3 + 4 +

On Track

After a short drum phrase, there is a 4-bar (16-beat) introduction. The structure is: chorus, verse, chorus, verse, chorus. There is an extra strum on F at the end.

page 11

Finger tips

- Remember to 'damp' or 'stop' the strings with the side of your strumming hand between each chord.

Challenge
- Try playing the second verse as a ukulele solo – this is written out for you on the TAB sheet, and can be heard on the demo track.

Samba Lele

Popping around
the world

(A samba song)

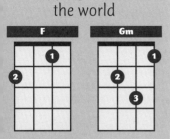

VERSE

F   Gm
In a favela in Rio,
C7   F
At the Escola de Samba,
F   Gm
Lele is singing and dancing,
C7   F
Ready for carnival time.

CHORUS

F   Gm
Samba, samba, samba Lele,
C7   F
Samba, samba, samb'oo-la-la.
F   Gm
Samba, samba, samba Lele,
C7   F
Samba, samba, samb'oo-la-la.

VERSE, INTRO & OUTRO
Two-bar samba strum

CHORUS
Calypso pattern with roll strum

On Track
The introduction starts with 8 bars of samba percussion before the progression (or sequence) of the first four chords of the song is played. The piece is played twice, ending with an outro on the 4-chord sequence.

Audio 8 (d)   Audio 9 (b)

Video A   Video B   Scores

Fingertips
- When playing percussion parts on the ukulele by slapping and tapping the body of the instrument, it is important to do this very gently to avoid damaging the ukulele or knocking the strings out of tune.
- (Teacher) A demonstration of the roll strum is shown in video clip A.

Challenge
- (Teacher) Try the ukulele percussion demonstrated in video clip B.
- Try playing the second verse, or even the whole thing, as a ukulele solo using the TAB sheet.

UNIT 3
STRUMATHONS & HIT PROGRESSIONS

Things to remember:

- The strumming patterns in the Strumathons are all index finger strums.

- As explained in Unit 1, strums in a 'straight' style are of equal length in a 'chug-ga, chug-ga, chug-ga, chug-ga' pattern, and in a 'swing' style, the down strums are played slightly longer in the 'doo-bee, doo-bee, doo-bee, doo-bee' pattern commonly found in jazz. This is the style used in the song 'Ukulele Boogie Woogie'.

TWO PIECES TO STRUM

Strumathon 1

Strumathon 2

In this section you will:

- Review and play a variety of strumming patterns we have learned so far
- Play strums in both 'swing' and 'straight' rhythm styles
- Learn more about harmony and chord progressions (sequences)
- Play two common chord progressions in three different keys

Good to know...

Harmony is a huge subject but there are a few things about it that are useful for a young ukulele player to understand:

Scales

A scale is a series of notes usually arranged in 8 regular steps, rising or falling in pitch, with the eighth note being the same as the first. For example, a C scale is:

1	2	3	4	5	6	7	8
C	D	E	F	G	A	B	C

Chords

A chord can be built up on each of the steps of a scale. For the purpose of harmony, each step is numbered using Roman numerals.

For example, chord II in the scale of C would be built on the note D (the second step in the C scale). Chord V in that scale would be built on the note G (the fifth step in the C scale).

Chord progressions (sequences)

When chords are played in a particular order, we call it a chord 'progression' or a chord 'sequence'.

page 13

Strumathons &
hit progressions

Strumathon 1

(Hit Progression 1, 'the 50s progression' – swing strums)

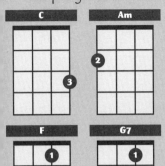

Chord progression I-VI-IV-V7 in three keys:

Progression	I	VI	IV	V7
Key of C major	C	Am	F	G7
Key of F major	F	Dm	B♭	C7
Key of G major	G	Em	C	D7

Fingertips

- Play all the strums in a 'swing' style.
- The chord diagrams for the key of C are displayed here – use the chord diagrams sheet (available online or by clicking on the 'Scores' icon) to help you play the progression in the keys of F and G.
- (Teacher) The video clip provides a demonstration (in C).

Strumming patterns

	1	&	2	&	3	&	4	&
Whole-bar	↓							
Half-bar	↓				↓			
Beat (pulse)	↓		↓		↓		↓	
Shuffle	↓	↑	↓	↑	↓	↑	↓	↑
Accented shuffle	↓	↑	↓	↑	↓	↑	↓	↑
Reggae 1			↓				↓	
Reggae 2			↓	↑			↓	
Calypso/Latin	↓		↓	↑		↑	↓	

On Track

There are three backing tracks: one for each key. The key for each track is indicated in the audio label, e.g. Audio 10 (C). There is a 4-bar (16-beat) introduction. Four beats on the bell signal the start of each new strumming pattern.

Challenge

- This progression has been used in many hit songs, especially in the 1950s, so it is sometimes referred to as the '50s progression'. But it has been used in other, more recent songs. Research and have a go at singing and playing some of the songs that feature this progression, such as: Baby (Justin Bieber), Dance With Me Tonight (Olly Murs), Eternal Flame (The Bangles), Every Breath You Take (The Police), I Will Always Love You (Dolly Parton/Whitney Houston), Stand By Me (Ben E. King), Total Eclipse Of The Heart (Bonnie Tyler).

Audio 10 (C) Audio 11 (F) Audio 12 (G)

Video Scores

Strumathon 2

(Hit Progression 2 – straight strums)

Chord progression I-V-VI-IV in three keys:

Progression	I	V	VI	IV
Key of C major	C	G	Am	F
Key of F major	F	C	Dm	B♭
Key of G major	G	D	Em	C

Fingertips

- Play all the strums in a 'swing' style.
- The chord diagrams for the key of C are displayed here – use the chord diagrams sheet (available online or by clicking on the 'Scores' icon) to help you play the progression in the keys of F and G.
- (Teacher) The video clip provides a demonstration (in C).

Strumming patterns

	1	&	2	&	3	&	4	&
Whole-bar	↓							
Half-bar	↓				↓			
Beat (pulse)	↓		↓		↓		↓	
Shuffle	↓	↑	↓	↑	↓	↑	↓	↑
Accented shuffle	↓	↑	↓	↑	↓	↑	↓	↑
Reggae 1			↓				↓	
Reggae 2			↓	↑			↓	
Calypso/Latin	↓		↓	↑		↑	↓	

On Track

There are three backing tracks: one for each key. The key for each track is indicated in the audio label, e.g. Audio 13 (C). There is a 4-bar (16-beat) introduction. Four beats on the bell signal the start of each new strumming pattern.

page 15

Audio 13 (C) Audio 14 (F)

Audio 15 (G) Video Scores

Challenge

- Like Hit Progression 1, this chord sequence has been used in lots of hit songs. It is the most commonly used chord progression in all forms of popular music. Try learning some of the songs that feature this progression, such as: Can You Feel The Love Tonight? (Elton John), Don't Stop Believin' (Journey/Glee cast), Let It Be (The Beatles), No Woman, No Cry (Bob Marley), Poker Face (Lady Gaga), Price Tag (Jessie J), She Will Be Loved (Maroon 5).
- Now you have learned some chord progressions that have produced many famous songs, why not try your hand at writing some songs yourself? Strum the progressions and see if any ideas for melodies or lyrics spring to mind.

UNIT 4
BALLADS OLD & NEW

Things to remember:

- It may help to refer to the song 'Leaving Home' in *Ukulele Magic: Tutor Book 1* – this is another ballad with a gentle, understated accompaniment.

TWO SONGS TO SING AND PLAY

Greensleeves

Star's End

In this section you will:

- Play a classic ballad from the Tudor period of British history
- Play a modern ballad based on the Christmas story
- Learn the new chord B♭ minor

Good to know...

- A ballad is a song, usually slow in tempo and reflective in nature, that tells a story or communicates the feelings of a character in a story.

- The lyrics of a ballad are important, so the accompaniment (backing) is usually kept simple to avoid distracting from the story being told in the song.

Greensleeves

Although it is over 500 years old, 'Greensleeves' is one of the most famous songs in the world. There was a theory that it was written by King Henry VIII about Anne Boleyn. Henry VIII did compose several songs of his own, notably 'Pastime With Good Company', but 'Greensleeves' did not appear until many years after the king died. It was discovered written on sheets of paper that were sold on the streets along with other popular ballads.

Star's End

'Star's End' was written as part of a nativity musical. It reflects on the long journey to Bethlehem of the Magi, sometimes referred to as the Three Wise Men or the Three Kings.

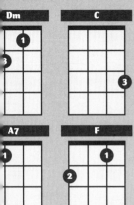

Greensleeves

(A famous Tudor ballad)

> Dm   C
> A-las, my love, you do me wrong
>
> Dm   A7
> To cast me off dis-courteously,
>
> Dm   C
> And I have loved you so long,
>
> Dm   A7   Dm
> De-lighting in your company.
>
> F   C
> Greensleeves was all my joy,
>
> Dm   A7
> Greensleeves was my delight,
>
> F   C
> Greensleeves was my heart of gold,
>
> Dm   A7   Dm
> And who but my lady Greensleeves.

On Track

There is a 2-bar (12-beat) drum and drone introduction followed by four D minor strums before the melody begins. The piece is played twice through.

Thumb brush strum

1   2

Challenge

- Add shape to this song by changing how loudly you play and sing – for example, the first four lines could be played quietly, and the last four lines could be slightly louder.

- Try playing the ukulele solo using the TAB sheet. It replaces the melody for the first four lines the second time (you can hear this on the demo track).

Audio 16 (d)   Audio 17 (b)

Scores

Fingertips

- Keep the accompaniment simple. There is no need for a rhythmical strumming pattern in a song like this: thumb brush strums marking the beat are sufficient and very much in character with this antique piece.

Star's End

(A Christmas ballad)

Chords: F, Dm, Gm, Bb, Bbm, C, C7, Am, G, G7

On Track
The introduction is 8 bars (32 beats) long. The structure is: Verse 1, Verse 2, Bridge, Verse 3, Bridge, Verse 3, Coda.

VERSES

Half-bar thumb brush strum

1 + 2 + 3 + 4 +

VERSE 1

    F   Dm   Gm   Bbm

The star is moving onward to show the way a-gain,

        F   G   Bb   G7   C   C7

And it seems as though we'll never know what's really at Star's End.

VERSE 2

    F   Dm   Gm   Bbm

We travel through the evening un-til it's light once more,

        F   G   Bb   C7   F

But with each new day it's as far away as on the night be-fore.

BRIDGE

Am   Dm   G7   Am

Crossing the icy river, climbing the mountain side.

Am   Dm

Where will the starlight lead us?

G7   C

How long have we to ride?

BRIDGE

Calypso strum

1 + 2 + 3 + 4 +

VERSE 3

    F   Dm   Gm   Bbm

The star is moving onward to show the way a-gain,

        F   G   Bb   G7   C

And it seems as though we'll never know what's really at Star's End.

CODA

Bbm F   G   Bb   Gm C7   F

Yes, it seems as though we'll never know what's really   at   Star's   End.

Audio 18 (d)   Audio 19 (b)   Scores

Challenge
- Learn the chords to the intro and outro using the TAB sheet.
- Try playing the second bridge as a ukulele solo using the TAB sheet.

UNIT 5
MORE FINGER PICKING TRICKS

Things to remember:

- In *Ukulele Magic: Tutor Book 1* we played some fingerstyle picking using the thumb and index finger in the songs 'Shortnin' Bread' and 'Starlight Star Bright'.

TWO PIECES TO PLAY

Inside Out Interlude

Clawhammer Swing

In this section you will:

- Learn the inside-outside fingerstyle using the thumb and index finger
- Learn the banjo-type 'clawhammer' style of fingerpicking using the thumb and index finger
- Learn the new chords C major 7, F minor, D minor 7 and E7, and a new fretting for the chord F major

Good to know...

- Ukulele players have adopted the classical Spanish guitar method for naming the picking fingers, using the letters *p, i, m, a*. These are the Spanish words, their abbreviations and the English translation:

  Pulgar (*p*) = thumb
  Indice (*i*) = index finger
  Medio (*m*) = middle finger
  Anular (*a*) = ring finger

- When the notes of a chord are picked out separately instead of being sounded simultaneously, it is sometimes referred to as playing 'broken chords' or 'arpeggios'.

- For the pieces in this section, you could simply strum the chords until you're ready to try the picking patterns.

Inside Out Interlude

Inside-outside picking with three fingers:

	p	i	p	m	p	i	p	m
String	3	2	4	1	3	2	4	1

Outside-inside picking with three fingers:

	m	p	i	p	m	p	i	p
String	4	1	2	3	4	1	2	3

Clawhammer Swing

Clawhammer picking with three fingers:

	i						
p			p	i	p	m	p
1							
String(s) 4			3	2	4	1	3

Inside Out Interlude

More finger picking tricks

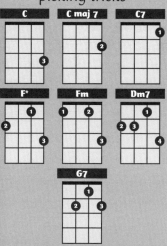

F* = alternative fretting for F major

(Instrumental)

Inside-outside pattern

	C				C maj 7			
String	3	2	4	1	3	2	4	1
	C7				F*			
String	3	2	4	1	3	2	4	1
	Fm				C			
String	3	2	4	1	3	2	4	1
	Dm7				G7			
String	3	2	4	1	3	2	4	1

Outside-inside pattern

	C				C maj 7				
String	1	4	2	3	1	4	2	3	
	C7				F*				
String	1	4	2	3	1	4	2	3	
	Fm				C				
String	1	4	2	3	1	4	2	3	
	Dm7				G7				C
String	1	4	2	3	1	4	2	3	*Strum*

On Track

There is a 2-bar (8-beat) introduction. The inside-outside pattern is played twice, then the outside-inside pattern is played once.

Fingertips

- To play fingerstyle, it is important to move the fingers but keep the hand still. Some ukulele players rest any non-picking fingers on the body of the ukulele below the strings to anchor their hand in position.

- (Teacher) You can use the demonstration videos to help you learn this piece. Video A shows the inside-outside pattern; video B shows the outside-inside pattern.

Challenge

- When you are confident, try playing the patterns double the speed, so that you play two patterns to every chord instead of one.

Audio 20 (d) **Audio 21 (b)**

Video A   Video B   Scores

Clawhammer Swing

More finger picking tricks

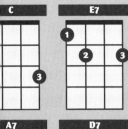
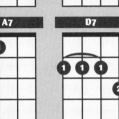

(Instrumental)

A SECTION

C	E7	A7	A7
/ / / /	/ / / /	/ / / /	/ / / /

D7	G7	C	G7 (C 2nd time)
/ / / /	/ / / /	/ / / /	/ / / /

Repeat A section

B SECTION

E7	E7	A7	A7
/ / / /	/ / / /	/ / / /	/ / / /

D7	D7	G7	G7
/ / / /	/ / / /	/ / / /	/ / / /

A SECTION

C	E7	A7	A7
/ / / /	/ / / /	/ / / /	/ / / /

D7	G7	C	C
/ / / /	/ / / /	/ / / /	/ / / /

Strum

On Track

There is a 2-bar (8-beat) drum and bass introduction to the piece.

page 21

Audio 22 (d) **Audio 23 (b)**
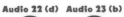

Video **Scores**

Finger tips

● If you find the clawhammer tricky, try it very slowly at first, using just one chord, and playing without the backing track. After a while, the finger pattern feels much more natural and you can concentrate on the chord changes and playing at a faster tempo.

● (Teacher) The video clip provides a demonstration of the pattern using the A section of the piece.

Challenge

● Try playing the melody using the TAB sheet.

● Write some lyrics to the melody to make a song.

● Play the piece without the backing track and try some new melodies of your own. You can start by humming along to come up with ideas.

UNIT 6
TRIPLE TIME

Things to remember:

- All the strumming patterns in the two Strumathons were organised in a metre of four beats (4/4), which is a very commonly used pattern in music – in fact, it is sometimes referred to as 'common time'.

- The song 'Daisy Bell' is in the triple metre (3/4), which requires a different kind of strumming pattern.

- The song 'Big Sad Wolf' is in a metre of 4 beats, but each individual beat is divided into three parts (also known as 'triplets'), which give the piece its 'ONE-and-a TWO-and-a THREE-and-a FOUR-and-a' pattern.

TWO SONGS TO SING AND PLAY

Daisy Bell

Big Sad Wolf

In this section you will:

- Learn the new chord F7
- Play a 3/4 waltz time strumming pattern
- Play the triple strum

Good to know...

The triple strum played with the thumb and index finger (p & i):

Tr   Tr   Tr   Tr

↓ ↓ ↑ ↓ ↓ ↑ ↓ ↓ ↑ ↓ ↓ ↑

i   *p*   *i*   *i*   *p*   *i*   *i*   *p*   *i*   *i*   *p*   *i*

1   +   a   2   +   a   3   +   a   4   +   a

Daisy Bell

Triple time

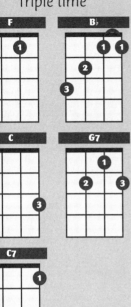

(A song in 3/4 triple metre)

F   F   B♭   F
Daisy, Daisy, give me your answer, do.

C   F   G7   C
I'm half crazy, all for the love of you.

  C7   F
It won't be a stylish marriage,

    F   B♭   F
I can't af-ford a carriage,

       F   C   F   C
But you'll look sweet up-on the seat

         F   C7   F
Of a bicycle built for two!

Waltz-style strum

1 + 2 + 3 +

On Track

There is a 4-bar (12-beat) introduction. The second verse is played as a ukulele solo.

page 23

Audio 24 (d)   Audio 25 (b)

Video   Scores

Finger tips

- When you play a three beat, waltz-style strum, put a slight accent on the first down strum in each group.

- (Teacher) The video clip shows how to play the waltz-style strum.

Challenge

- This song works well as a ukulele solo – it lies comfortably in 1st position on the fretboard. Use the TAB sheet to give it a go.

Big Sad Wolf

Triple time

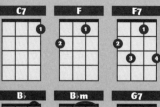
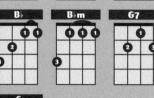
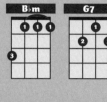

(A song with triple strums)

Introduction

F   B♭   F

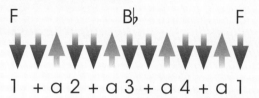

1 + a 2 + a 3 + a 4 + a 1

Swing accented shuffle strum
(Ukulele solo second time)

                 C7   F

It makes me wanna howl, it makes me wanna howl,

              C7   C7

There's nothing I can do, there's nothing I can say,

           F   F7

To help me try to keep the blues a-way.

Triple strum
(Sing both times)

Swing accented shuffle strum

1 + a 2 + a 3 + a 4 + a

             B♭   B♭

'Cause when I look up at the moon a-bove me,

          F   F

It makes me wonder why I got no-one to love me.

   G7   G7

I know that I've been bad, that's why I'm feeling sad,

   C   C7

I wish that I could turn my life a-round.

On Track

- There is a short, 2-bar introduction, which could be played with the triple strum on chords F and B♭ in a live performance.

- The piece is played twice, and the last two lines are repeated at the end.

Triple strum on 1 and 3

1 + a 2 + a 3 + a 4 + a

Audio 26 (d)   **Audio 27 (b)**   **Video**   **Scores**

Big Sad Wolf (continued)

(A song with triple strums)

Swing accented shuffle strum

N.C.   F   F7   Bb

You see that, in the end,   I'm just a wolf without a friend,

Bbm   F   C

    And so I sit and sigh, it makes me wanna cry,

                                   F

It makes me wanna howl!

(Second time only)

Bbm   F   C

    And so I sit and sigh, it makes me wanna cry,

                          F   Bb   F

It makes me wanna howl!

Fingertips

- (Teacher) A demonstration of the triple strum is shown in the video clip.
- You could play the triple strum for every beat on the lyric 'I wish that I could turn…'

Challenge

- Try the solo ukulele verse using the TAB sheet.
- Add the harmony part (also on the TAB sheet) if you have two or more players.

UNIT 7
MOVING MUSIC

Things to remember:

- You have now learned to play a range of new chords. In this unit, you can use these chords to play music in several different keys.

Good to know...

Moving chords & chord diagrams

- Most chords where you fret all four strings in a particular chord 'shape' can be shifted up the fretboard to create a different, higher pitched chord. Instead of drawing very tall chord diagrams to indicate chords located higher up the fretboard, we use the usual size diagram, but with a fret label, for example:

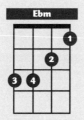
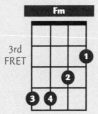

Moving tunes & scales

- Most tunes or scales that you have mastered in one key can be moved to a different position on the fretboard to play them in a higher key.

page 26

- For 'Hard Times Blues', the melody and blues scale are moved from 2nd position (where the first finger is located over the 2nd fret) for the version in D, to 4th position (where the first finger is located over the 4th fret) for the version in E.

THREE SONGS TO SING AND PLAY

Hard Times Blues
(in D and E)

Everybody Loves
Saturday Night

Good King Wenceslas

In this section you will:

- Play and sing songs that change ('modulate') from one key to another
- Learn about choosing a suitable key for a melody
- Learn some melody shapes and chord shapes that can be moved to different parts of the fretboard
- Improvise using the D and E blues scales
- Play the new chord B7
- Play the new chords C5 and G5 to create the characteristic 'drone' sound associated with medieval music

Moving keys

- The key of a particular piece of music could be chosen for many different reasons. One key might be uncomfortably high for a singer, or too low to play on an instrument like the ukulele, where the lowest pitched note is 'middle C' (about halfway up the keyboard on a piano).

- When a key is changed for a piece, both the melody and the associated chords need to be changed. When the key is changed for a whole piece, as in the case of 'Hard Times Blues', we call it a 'transposition'. When the key is changed *during* a piece of music, as in 'Everybody Loves Saturday Night' and 'Good King Wenceslas', we call it a 'modulation'.

Hard Times Blues

Moving music

ords I7, IV7 and V7
in the key of D

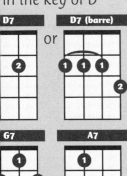

(A blues song to improvise in the key of D)

D7	D7	D7	D7

Hard times, hard times, how long are you gonna stay?

G7	G7	D7	D7

Hard times, hard times, how long are you gonna stay?

A7	G7	D7	D7

Stick around much longer, and I'll be going on my way.

Strumming pattern

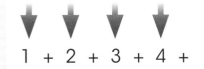

1 + 2 + 3 + 4 +

TAB FOR D BLUES SCALE

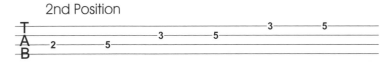

On Track

- There is a 2-bar (8-beat) introduction.

- The piece is played 3 times (3 verses). The second verse on the demo track is an example of a solo.

page 27

Audio 28 (d)   Audio 29 (b)

Video   Scores

Fingertips

- This piece works well with simple down strums. They will sound more jazzy if you make them short by damping the strings.

- The solo is played in 2nd position (with the first finger located over the 2nd fret).

Challenge

- Try improvising a solo for the second verse using the D blues scale.

- (Teacher) The video clip provides an example solo.

- Try learning the melody using the TAB sheet.

- You could add some improvised vocal phrases to the last verse, as heard on the demo track.

Unit 7

Moving music

Chords I7, IV7 and V7 in the key of E

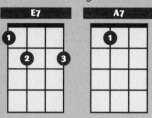

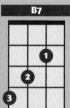

More Hard Times Blues

(A blues song to improvise in the key of E)

E7	E7	E7	E7

Hard times, hard times, how long are you gonna stay?

A7	A7	E7	E7

Hard times, hard times, how long are you gonna stay?

B7	A7	E7	E7

Stick around much longer, and I'll be going on my way.

Strumming pattern

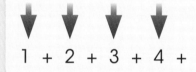

1 + 2 + 3 + 4 +

TAB FOR E BLUES SCALE

4th Position

```
T|--------------------------------5-------7--
A|----4--------7--------5----7----------------
B|--------------------------------------------
```

On Track

- There is a 2-bar (8-beat) introduction.
- The piece is played 3 times (3 verses).

Fingertips

- Use the same down strums as in 'Hard Times Blues'.
- The solo is played in 4th position (with the first finger located over the 4th fret).

Challenge

- Try improvising a solo for the second verse using the E blues scale.
- (Teacher) The video clip provides an example solo in D (2nd position). The same shapes would work for E, just move to 4th position.
- Try learning the melody using the TAB sheet.
- You could add some improvised vocal phrases to the last verse, as heard on the demo track.

Audio 30 (d) Audio 31 (b)

Video

Scores

Everybody Loves Saturday Night

(A traditional Afro-Caribbean song modulating to a different key)

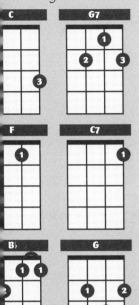

1st time: C major, 2nd time: F major

C	G7	C	C
F	C7	F	F

Everybody loves Saturday night,

C	G7	C	C
F	C7	F	F

Everybody loves Saturday night,

C	F	C	G
F	B♭	F	C

Everybody,   everybody, everybody, everybody,

C	G7	C	C7
F	C7	F	F

Everybody loves Saturday night.

Calypso strum

1 + 2 + 3 + 4 +

On Track

There is a 4-bar (16-beat) introduction. The piece is played twice: once in C major and once in F major.

page 29

Audio 32 (d)   Audio 33 (b)

Scores

Finger tips

- Try adding a roll strum on beat 2 of the calypso pattern (as used in 'Samba Lele' on page 12.

Challenge

- Learn to play the second verse (in the key of F major) using the TAB sheet.

Good King Wenceslas

(A traditional Christmas carol modulating to a different key)

Introduction

G5
C5

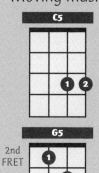

C5

G5
2nd
FRET

G5   G5
C5   C5
Good King Wenceslas looked out, on the Feast of Stephen;

G5   G5
C5   C5
When the snow lay round about, deep and crisp, and even:

G5   G5
C5   C5
Brightly shone the moon that night, though the frost was cruel,

G5   G5   G5
C5   C5   C5
When a poor man came in sight, gathering winter fuel.

On Track

There is a 4-bar (8-beat) introduction before the drone pattern begins, and a further 4 bars (four strums) before the melody comes in. Four strums are played on C5 as an introduction to the second verse.

Thumb brush strum (drone)

1   +   2   +

Fingertips

- Play the drone part with thumb brush strums.
- This piece is in 2/4 metre (there are two beats in every bar).
- Song structure: Play the piece once through in G, then go straight back to the beginning, changing to C. Use the drone strum for the G verse, then try the other parts for the C verse.
- (Teacher) The video shows how all the parts fit together.

Audio 34 (d)   Audio 35 (b)

Video

Scores

Good King Wenceslas second verse melody

(A traditional Christmas carol modulating to a different key)

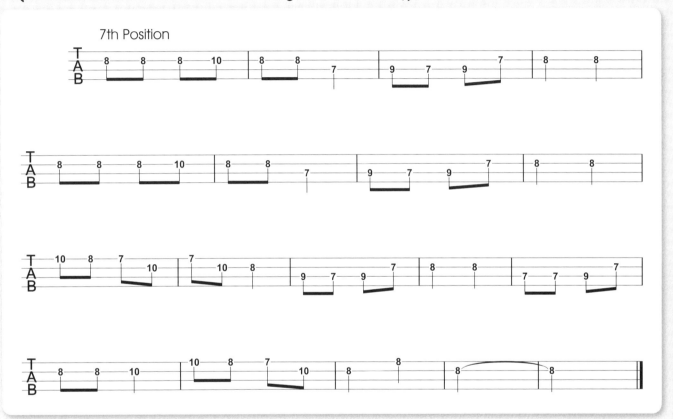

Challenge

- The melody part for the whole piece is provided on the TAB sheet. Play this for both verses for an instrumental version, or just for the second verse (given here) if the first verse is sung.

Good King Wenceslas second verse harmony

(A traditional Christmas carol modulating to a different key)

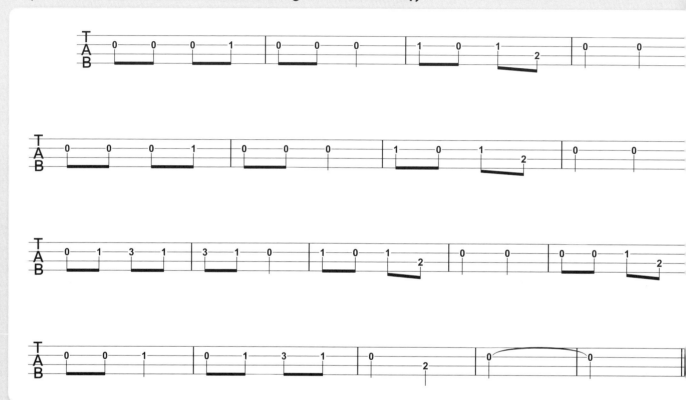

Challenge

- Try adding this optional harmony part for the second verse. For a live performance you could add a drum (or play the rhythm on a ukulele). The ukulele parts could also be played on recorders or flutes.